THE
JERSEY EASTERN
RAILWAY
and the
German Occupation Lines
in Jersey

by
N. R. P. Bonsor

THE OAKWOOD PRESS

© Oakwood Press 1986

First Published 1965
First Reprint 1973
Second Revised Edition 1977
Third Reprint 1981
Fourth Reprint 1986

ISBN 0 85361 345 1

Printed by S & Press, Abingdon, Oxford

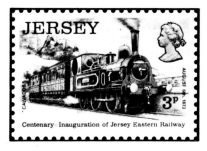

Stamps issued to Commemorate the Centenary of the Jersey Eastern Railway.

Published by
THE OAKWOOD PRESS
P.O. Box 122,
Headington, Oxford

This book forms a continuation of the
same author's "Jersey Railway (J.R. & T.)"
published by The Oakwood Press and the page
numbers follow on from it.

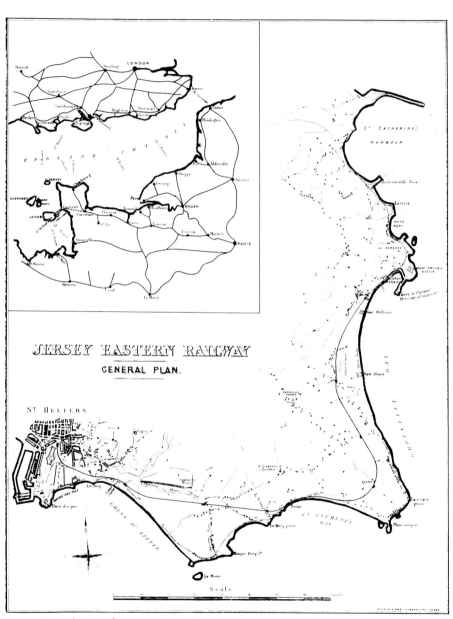

Reproduction of rare map circa 1880, showing J.E.R. open to Gorey Village and
extension contemplated to Gorey Pier (completed 1891) and St. Catherine's Bay
(abandoned). Note the contractor's lines leading to Archirondelle (sic!) Tower and to
St. Catherine's Breakwater, the second arm of which was never built

Jersey Eastern Railway Company Limited

THE Bill authorising the construction of the Jersey Railway along the south coast of the Island from St. Helier to St. Aubin was, as is stated in Volume I, confirmed by Her Majesty in Council on 22 October 1869 and the line was opened almost exactly a year later. The volume of traffic during the first few weeks more than came up to expectations and it is not surprising therefore, that on 18 January 1871 the Constable of St. Helier presented a petition to the States of Jersey on behalf of the projectors of a railway to run between St. Helier and Gorey, on the east coast, to be known as the Jersey Eastern Railway. The *projet de loi* was lodged *au Greffe* and came up for discussion on 15 March 1871. By a coincidence, a petition in respect of a third railway to run between St. Aubin and La Moye came before the States on the very same day.

The preamble of the Jersey Eastern Railway Bill was approved on 16 March 1871 and the Bill as a whole was considered by the House on the 31st of the same month. There had, of course, been precedents in the Jersey Railway's unsuccessful Bill of 1863 and the same company's successful Bill of 1869. In consequence, there was much in common between the 67 articles of the latter and the 68 articles of the new Bill in the name of the Jersey Eastern Railway Company, Limited, the following being a summary of some of the most important or interesting of these articles:—

Article 3. The capital was stated to be £40,000 in shares of £5 each.

Article 4. In the event of the extension of the line being carried out from Gorey to St. Catherine's the capital could be increased by a sum not exceeding £20,000 subject to agreement at a general meeting.

Article 45. The railway was authorised from Snow Hill, in the parish of St. Helier, to Gorey and from there to St. Catherine's Bay.

Article 46. The railway might consist of a single line or of more than one set of rails. The service was to be carried out by means of locomotives. There was no mention of gauge.

Article 47 made provision for access to shipyards along the route—whether already existing or built at some later date.

Article 54 stipulated that in the event of disagreement over any property situated within the limits indicated on the plans, the claimant could not cause work to cease by raising the *Clameur de Haro*. The complaint must be lodged with the Royal Court for consideration and decision as soon as possible.

Article 55 fixed a maximum fare between St. Helier and Gorey of 1½*d.* a mile or fraction of a mile first class and 1*d.* a mile or fraction of a mile second class.

Article 59 stated that there must be a minimum of four services a day in each direction between St. Helier and Gorey. If the company failed to provide a full service during 60 or more days in the course of a year—except on Sundays, or when the line was out of action owing to necessary repairs, or unless permission had been granted by the Main Roads Committee—the Company would be considered to have abandoned the enterprise and the States would be empowered to take possession of the railway, buildings, etc., without recourse to the paying of compensation.

Article 61 stated that construction of the line between St. Helier and Gorey must be completed and the service put into operation within three years of the registration of the relevant Order in Council; and that the remainder of the line must be completed within ten years.

Article 68 empowered the States at any time they thought fit to purchase the railway by repaying the company their costs of construction plus 33⅓ per cent.

The committee appointed by the States to examine the proposed line of the railway met on 15 May 1871 in order to hear those owners of land who wished to raise objections. About a dozen people appeared before the committee, but only four or five objected strongly to the railway passing through their property and the remainder said that they would be satisfied if they received fair compensation.

The committee's report together with plans and specifications came before the States on 21 June 1871. The Bill was approved and the Greffier was instructed to forward it as quickly as possible to the Privy Council for confirmation. This was granted on 19 March 1872.

It was announced on 1 May 1872 that workmen had started to build fences at places in the parish of St. Clement and that within a few days work would commence all along the line. On 12 June the schooner *Emma* arrived at St. Helier from Cardiff with the necessary contractor's plant and almost at once digging commenced in Green Street and at Le Hocq. A fortnight later the navvies stopped work and demanded an increase in pay of 6d. a day and a reduction in daily hours of work to ten. The contractor, having only a limited time in which to complete his contract and being liable to a severe penalty clause, considered that he had no alternative but to agree to the demands of the strikers, who hitherto had been paid 3s. a day in the case of the key men, and the remainder according to their capabilities. The contractor let it be known that if any further trouble arose he would obtain labour from England.

On 17 September 1872 Mrs. Edward Mourant, wife of the chairman of the Board of Directors, dug the first turf at a private ceremony which was attended solely by personal friends of the directors. To commemorate the occasion Mr. and Mrs. Mourant were presented with a wheelbarrow *ornée de sculptures élégantes* and a silver spade.* Elsewhere by this time, considerable progress had been made and in many places the rails, sleepers, fishplates and spikes had been placed beside the line in readiness for assembly.

By the end of November the abutments for an iron bridge crossing Roseville Street were already complete, and rails had been laid on the embankment from Green Street to that point. The next step was to make use of temporary wooden beams until such time as the ironwork of the bridge was ready to be installed so that the permanent way could be continued as far as the Dicq. At Green Street an engine shed was being built and also a temporary station as it was probable that the permanent terminus behind Fort Regent would not be ready for another year.

---

* These are now on view at the Jersey Museum, Pier Road, St. Helier.

At a meeting held at the beginning of March 1873 it was decided to allow the contractor, Mr. Baldwin, until 1 May to complete the works and not to put into operation until then the heavy penalty that was due to apply in the event of the non-completion of the line by 1 March. The weather had been so bad since the previous September that work had been totally suspended during nearly a third of the time.

The steamer *Staperayder* arrived at St. Helier on 15 April with two passenger carriages for the railway, these being the forerunners of an expected total of 20. On the same day it was announced that the President of the French Republic had given his approval to the building of the Carteret and Carentan Railway, and the view was expressed that the line would be of great benefit to the Jersey Eastern Railway as well as to the Island in general. As shown in Volume I several years elapsed before the French line was opened for traffic.

Two days later a sensation was caused when it became known that Mr. Baldwin had informed the workmen, when they turned up for work at 6 a.m., that their services would no longer be required and that if they went along to the office they would be paid up to and including that day. No reason was given for this suspension, but it was understood that the railway company did not owe Mr. Baldwin any arrears of money. It was announced on 5 May that possession of the line had been surrendered to the company and that the directors were determined to continue the works immediately.

In the meanwhile, on 27 April 1873 the sailing ship *Emma* arrived at St. Helier with two locomotives which, three days later, proceeded with much difficulty to the new engine shed at Green Street. No details were given of the route taken, but it is more than likely that it was the same as that selected for a transfer many years later, namely, via Mulcaster Street, Colomberie and Grenville Street. Preliminary trials of the engines took place on 22 May and were considered to have been most satisfactory. The builders were Kitson & Co., of Leeds, the cost about £1,800 each and the engines were named *Caesarea* and *Calvados*. For the benefit of readers unfamiliar with the Channel Islands, Caesarea is the Roman name for Jersey and Calvados a Department in Normandy. The latter choice indicates the high hopes of the Jersey directors regarding the projected French line.

A few days later the company drew the attention of the public in newspaper advertisements to the danger of walking on the track and stated that the directors would not be responsible for any accident arising therefrom. The line was already complete as far as Pontac and the engines were being used extensively for transporting ballast and other materials from one section to another.

Two further passenger carriages arrived by the s.s. *Staperayder* at the beginning of June and another two at the end of that month. They were stated to weigh between four and five tons, to be larger and stronger than those of the Jersey Railway and were described as not-very-elegant boxes on wheels. It was further stated that they were fitted with brakes operating in a very simple manner and very effectively but no technical details were given.

A somewhat mysterious announcement was made at this time that "a portion of the rails placed temporarily between Green Street and Roseville Street are being taken up and will be replaced by other permanent ones, on a totally different system". There are various possible explanations, one being that the temporary rails were laid on longitudinal sleepers with tie-rods, as on the G.W.R., whereas the permanent arrangement was to have the standard type of sleeper, to which the flat-bottomed rails were spiked direct.

The first mishap on the line was of a totally unexpected nature and happened during the lunch hour on 26 June 1873 when one of the carriages which had just arrived at Green Street from the harbour started off under its own momentum down the steep incline, demolishing two crossing gates and finishing up somewhere in the direction of Grève d'Azette. Fortunately no one was hurt and it was stated that precautions had been taken to prevent a recurrence.

At 8 a.m. on 2 July 1873 a special train consisting of a locomotive and 14 trucks each loaded with two tons or more of stone and ballast left Green Street and proceeded to Grouville and back in order to test the solidarity of the permanent way and bridges. This preliminary trial being satisfactory, at 12-30 p.m. the Main Roads Committee, accompanied by the company's chairman and engineer, left Green Street in a train consisting of an engine and two passenger carriages for the same destination as earlier. In general, the committee approved of the works, the crossings and bridges, but indicated one or two minor changes which they felt should be carried out. It only remained for the final inspection by the engineer appointed by the States before the railway could be opened to the public.

On the afternoon of 9 July a party of the company's guests proceeded from Green Street to Grouville and back. There was a slight mishap at the conclusion of the return journey as it appears that the engine overshot by about 20 yards the point where it was intended to stop and reached a spot where the rails, although laid, had not been properly secured. In consequence, the engine was derailed and collided gently with a newly-arrived carriage, which was being placed on the line. Only trifling damage was done.

Some extensive army manoeuvres had been arranged to take place on Grouville Common on 10 July 1873, the troops concerned belonging to three local regiments and two batteries of artillery. The Jersey Eastern Railway generously offered to transport the St. Helier battalion free of charge by train (it would, of course, have been illegal to accept them as fare-paying passengers as the line had not been inspected and approved); and this offer being gratefully accepted the men arrived at the station shortly after 3 a.m. The embarkation of the troops took place without hitch, and "the enormous train was set in motion with its load of nearly 700 persons". A large crowd awaited the arrival of the train at the Wimbledon Hotel, which was then the terminus of the line.

The States met on the morning of 6th August to hear the report of Mr. Imrie Bell, c.e., the engineer appointed by them to inspect the line. It stated that the line was a single one, 5¼ miles long, built to a gauge of 4 feet 8½ inches, and that the gradients and curves were easy and moderate. "So long as the single line was worked there was no necessity for signals; but it was the intention of the directors to work the line on the block system by telegraph and the communication would be carried into effect shortly." The Constable of St. Clement, Mr. Edward Mourant, who was also chairman of the railway, stated that Mr. Bell's report applied only to the portion between Green Street and Grouville stations and that the portion between Grouville and Gorey would be completed within a few days. He suggested and it was agreed that the production of Mr. Bell's certificate and the sanction of the President of the States should be full authority for the opening of the additional section.

At the conclusion of the session, the members of the States proceeded to Green Street station, where they were received by the company's directors. They then boarded the train of six carriages which were already occupied by the ladies invited to the ceremony. Although the train stopped at all except the first and last of the intermediate stations of George Town (sic!), Samarès, Le Hocq, Pontac, La Rocque and Les Marais, it reached Grouville station, situated almost opposite the Wimbledon Hotel, in 15 minutes. Arrived at their destination, the guests were entertained under the shelter of a marquee "with music outside and refreshment within" and after "an exchange of congratulations" returned to town at 5 p.m. It was not nearly such a formal ceremony as the one three years earlier at the opening of the Jersey Railway, but as there was much less speech-making it was probably much more enjoyable!

The stations at George Town and Les Marais were built of wood and were not quite complete; it was stated that they would be opened within about a week. The others were of stone, with brickwork quoins and dressings round the windows and doors, and were covered with blue plastering after the fashion of stations in Normandy, Mr. H. G. Hammond Spencer, the company's engineer, having received some of his training in France. With the exception of George Town and Samarès, the stations contained booking offices, ladies' waiting rooms, general waiting rooms, and houses for the stationmasters. All the intermediate stations except Pontac had a single platform but here there were two platforms and a crossing loop. At a later date Grouville also had two lines and platforms, but whether the second existed to begin with is not certain. The railway passed over two iron bridges—"one at Roseville Street and one in Mr. De Quetteville's field near Green Street, and over a wooden one at Le Hocq". The second bridge was across what we now know as Cleveland Road. At Le Hocq there was also a cutting and a bridge under the coast road leading to Pontac, where the railway ran along the sea shore and where a vast expanse of rocks was exposed at low tide. Mont Orgueil castle at Gorey came into view on approaching La Rocque station. Near Grouville station were the race course, rifle range and golf links.

Advertisements stated that the line would be opened to the public on 7 August 1873, and that until further notice the trains would run as follows:—

"From St. Helier's to Grouville hourly, from 8 a.m. to 1 p.m., again at 2-30 p.m., hourly from 4 p.m. to 7 p.m., and another train at 8-30 p.m. From Grouville to St. Helier's hourly from 8-30 a.m. to 12-30 p.m., again at 2 o'clock, and hourly from 3-30 p.m. until 7-30 p.m., when there will be none between that time and the last train at 9 o'clock."

Subsequent reports said that nearly all the trains on the opening day were well-filled. It was also stated that "the oscillation of the train when in motion is extremely little, indeed scarcely perceptible".

The first mishap after the public opening took place only one day later, on 8 August, when the 9 a.m. train from St. Helier "got off the line on turning the curve at the side of Pontac". No damage was done and traffic was resumed at 1 o'clock.

On the second and subsequent Saturdays an additional train left Green Street at 10 p.m. for Grouville, returning at 10-30 p.m. The extension to Gorey was opened on 27 August, on and after which date all trains terminated there instead of at Grouville. The fête of the Good Templars and the Rechabites was held at Gorey on 1 September and on that occasion over 2,500 excursionists were carried by the railway.

The new terminus at Snow Hill was opened on 6 May 1874 and consisted of a single-sided platform with one running road and two carriage sidings; the Green Street terminus was closed simultaneously.

In 1876 Mr. John Wimble, the secretary and manager, retired and was succeeded by Mr. Edward Le Quesne. It was decided at this time to issue cheap return tickets on Sunday afternoons from St. Helier or George Town to Gorey or intermediate stations for 6*d*. The ordinary return fare to Grouville or Gorey was 10*d*. second class and 1*s*. or 1*s*.2*d*. respectively first, cheaper rates being in operation for the intermediate stations. On Good Friday and Easter Monday 1876 return tickets between any two stations were issued at a fare of 6*d*.

Wednesday and Thursday, 21 and 22 June 1876 were busy days for the company owing to the summer horse races on Gorey Common.

A total of 28 trains left St. Helier on each day, including seven at 20-minute intervals between 11 a.m. and 1 p.m.

Readers of Volume I will be aware that the Jersey Railway was declared *en désastre* in December 1874. No details are available concerning the financial results of the Jersey Eastern Railway during the years 1873-75 inclusive, but one does at least know that it managed to steer clear of bankruptcy. In 1876 the traffic receipts were £4,541 and in 1877 £4,860. Debenture interest was paid in both years, and it seems that interest on the 5 per cent preference shares was paid for the first half of 1876 but not again until 1881 or later. It follows that there was no ordinary dividend during this period.

It was reported in December 1880 that telegraphic communication had been established between St. Helier, Pontac, Grouville and Gorey. A few weeks earlier telephones had been installed temporarily pending the arrival of the telegraphic apparatus from the Silvertown India

Jersey Eastern Railway Company, Limited.

1875.

SUMMER SERVICE.

STATIONS.	DOWN: WEEK DAYS.											Wednesdays and Saturdays only.	DOWN. SUNDAYS.							
	a.m.	a.m.	a.m.	a.m.	p.m.	p.m.	p.m.	p.m.	p.m.	p.m.	p.m.	p.m.	a.m.	p.m.	p.m.	p.m.	p.m.	p.m.	p.m.	p.m.
ST. HELIER (dep.)	8 0	9 0	10 15	11 30	1 0	2 30	3 30	4 30	5 30	7 0	8 30	9 45	9 30	1 0	2 30	3 30	4 30	5 30	7 0	8 30
GEORGE TOWN...	8 3	9 3	10 18	11 33	1 3	2 33	3 33	4 33	5 33	7 3	8 33	9 48	9 33	1 3	2 33	3 33	4 33	5 33	7 3	8 33
SAMARÈS........	8 5	9 5	10 20	11 35	1 5	2 35	3 35	4 35	5 35	7 5	8 35	9 50	9 35	1 5	2 35	3 35	4 35	5 35	7 5	8 35
LE HOCQ........	8 8	9 8	10 23	11 38	1 8	2 38	3 38	4 38	5 38	7 8	8 38	9 53	9 38	1 8	2 38	3 38	4 38	5 38	7 8	8 38
PONTAC	8 10	9 10	10 25	11 40	1 10	2 40	3 40	4 40	5 40	7 10	8 40	9 55	9 40	1 10	2 40	3 40	4 40	5 40	7 10	8 40
LA ROCQUE......	8 14	9 14	10 29	11 44	1 14	2 44	3 44	4 44	5 44	7 14	8 44	9 59	9 44	1 14	2 44	3 44	4 44	5 44	7 14	8 44
LES MARAIS	8 17	9 17	10 32	11 47	1 17	2 47	3 47	4 47	5 47	7 17	8 47	10 2	9 47	1 17	2 47	3 47	4 47	5 47	7 17	8 47
GROUVILLE......	8 19	9 19	10 34	11 49	1 19	2 49	3 49	4 49	5 49	7 19	8 49	10 4	9 49	1 19	2 49	3 49	4 49	5 49	7 19	8 49
GOREY (arr.)......	8 22	9 22	10 37	11 52	1 22	2 52	3 52	4 52	5 52	7 22	8 52	10 7	9 52	1 22	2 52	3 52	4 52	5 52	7 22	8 52

STATIONS.	UP. WEEK DAYS.											Wednesdays and Saturdays only.	UP. SUNDAYS.							
	a.m.	a.m.	a.m.	noon.	p.m.	p.m.	p.m.	p.m.	p.m.	p.m.	p.m.	p.m.	a.m.	p.m.	p.m.	p.m.	p.m.	p.m.	p.m.	p.m.
GOREY (dep.)	8 30	9 30	10 45	12 0	1 45	3 0	4 0	5 0	6 0	7 45	9 0	10 15	10 15	1 30	3 0	4 0	5 0	6 0	7 30	9 0
GROUVILLE	8 33	9 33	10 48	12 3	1 48	3 3	4 3	5 3	6 3	7 48	9 3	10 18	10 18	1 33	3 3	4 3	5 3	6 3	7 33	9 3
LES MARAIS	8 35	9 35	10 50	12 5	1 50	3 5	4 5	5 5	6 5	7 50	9 5	10 20	10 20	1 35	3 5	4 5	5 5	6 5	7 35	9 5
LA ROCQUE	8 38	9 38	10 53	12 8	1 53	3 8	4 8	5 8	6 8	7 53	9 8	10 23	10 23	1 38	3 8	4 8	5 8	6 8	7 38	9 8
PONTAC	8 42	9 42	10 57	12 14	1 57	3 12	4 12	5 12	6 12	7 57	9 12	10 27	10 27	1 42	3 12	4 12	5 12	6 12	7 42	9 12
LE HOCQ	8 44	9 44	10 59	12 14	1 59	3 14	4 14	5 14	6 14	7 59	9 14	10 29	10 29	1 44	3 14	4 14	5 14	6 14	7 44	9 14
SAMARÈS	8 47	9 47	11 2	12 17	2 2	3 17	4 17	5 17	6 17	8 2	9 17	10 32	10 32	1 47	3 17	4 17	5 17	6 17	7 47	9 17
GEORGE TOWN ...	8 49	9 49	11 4	12 19	2 4	3 19	4 19	5 19	6 19	8 4	9 19	10 34	10 34	1 49	3 19	4 19	5 19	6 19	7 49	9 19
ST. HELIER (arr.)...	8 52	9 52	11 7	12 22	2 7	3 22	4 22	5 22	6 22	8 7	9 22	10 37	10 37	1 52	3 22	4 22	5 22	6 22	7 52	9 22

PRINTED AT THE "BRITISH PRESS & JERSEY TIMES" OFFICE, 29, HALKETT PLACE.

Rubber, Gutta Percha, and Telegraph Works Company Limited. They gave such "surprising satisfaction that most of the officials are very sorry to have to exchange them for the much slower and more troublesome means of transmitting their messages, and to be obliged to listen to the clicking of the signalling needle instead of the familiar voice of their fellow officials". The total cost of the installation was stated to be only £47 12s. 6d.

The principal events of the year 1881 were the opening of the Carteret—Carentan Railway and the introduction of steam communication between Carteret and Gorey by the Compagnie Rouennaise de Navigation.

At the annual general meeting held on 1 February 1884 a dividend of 5 per cent was declared on the preference shares and 1½ per cent on the ordinary shares. This was a red letter day in the history of the company as it marked the first payment of an ordinary dividend.

Although through tickets were issued between all stations on the Jersey Eastern Railway (and for that matter on the Jersey Railways Company Limited—as it had then become—in conjunction with the J.E.R.) and Paris, and the principal stations on the Western and the Northern Railways of France, via Gorey and thence steamer and rail, the transfer arrangements at Gorey were far from satisfactory owing to the distance of Gorey station from the steamer pier. On 25 May 1891 the railway was extended from what became known as Gorey Village station to a new terminus, about half a mile distant, at the approach to Gorey Pier. The line ran between a newly-built coast road and the sea wall.

The new station platform was 300 feet in length, the accompanying buildings containing "every convenience for the public in the shape of waiting rooms, shelters, etc.". There was a single platform line together with a run around loop.

The complete schedule of stopping trains from Snow Hill was now: George Town (3 mins.), Samarès (6 mins.), Le Hocq (8 mins.), Pontac (10 mins.), La Rocque (14 mins.), Les Marais (17 mins.), Grouville (19 mins.), Gorey Village (22 mins.) and Gorey Pier (24 mins). The ordinary return fare from St. Helier to Gorey Pier was 1s. 3d. first class and 1s. second class as compared with 1s. 1d. and 10d. respectively to Gorey

Village. The summer timetable, effective on 1 July 1891, showed 15 trains for the throughout journey in each direction on weekdays and nine on Sundays, all stopping at each intermediate station, but in addition there were on Sundays three fast trains from St. Helier to Gorey Pier and four in the reverse direction, stopping only at Pontac and Gorey Village. It is believed that this arrangement was not in operation during subsequent summers.

Two new stations, named St. Luke's and Grève d'Azette, were opened on 1 June 1896 and the former enabled the station at George Town (*sic*) to be closed. Up to World War I Grève d'Azette station was much patronised by people attending events at the cycle track and in consequence, although there was only one platform, there was a passing loop as at Don Bridge on the J.R. & T. From time to time special trains ran to Samarès in connection with fêtes at Samarès Manor, and in such cases the trains would be backed from Samarès to Grève d'Azette, where the engine would run around the train.

At the 26th annual general meeting held in February 1897 the chairman, Mr. Edward Mourant, who held this post until his death in 1899, commented that Grève d'Azette station, "standing in the open as it does for the present, bids fair to accommodate an increasing population". In the account of the general meeting, the *Jersey Times* referred to "this flourishing company", which it undoubtedly was as a dividend of 4 per cent was paid on the ordinary shares and £500 was placed in reserve. The profit and loss account showed receipts of £8,392 and expenditure of £6,121, leaving a net balance of £2,271.

The chairman also referred to improvements that were taking place at Snow Hill terminus, where the narrowness of the one and only platform seriously restricted the movement of passengers at times of pressure. A satisfactory solution had been found by quarrying as far back as possible the eastern wall of rock—that is to say, on the side furthest away from Fort Regent, and by reducing the three lines of rails to two—leaving, in other words, one platform line and one siding. In addition, a contract valued at £1,500 had been awarded a Liverpool firm for the erection of a station roof nearly 200 feet in length.

Finally, Mr. Mourant stated that the continental traffic was assuming larger and larger dimensions and must be fostered. A new steamer specially designed for the Carteret—Gorey service was in course of construction at Nantes. Although he did not mention this, H.M.S. *Raven* acted for many years as guardship at Gorey and her crew were a welcome source of passenger revenue for the company.

In January 1906 a J.E.R. petition was laid before the States of Jersey, asking for more extensive powers and, *inter alia*, the right to run electric cars. Jurat Le Gros pointed out that the company already possessed some of the powers asked for as he remembered quite well that in the original Bill the words "steam power" were purposely left out so that any other motive power might be used. It may be added that the Jersey Railways & Tramways Ltd., the successors to the Jersey Railways Company Limited, had discussed the question of electricity as long previously as 1897.

Mont Orgueil Castle was handed over by the British Government to the States on 28 June 1907 and on that occasion 1,800 troops left Snow Hill for Gorey in the space of 1½ hours. The train service for the general public ran at 20-minute intervals from 9 a.m. to 11 a.m. The number of passengers, including troops but exclusive of season ticket holders, carried during the day was 6,251, a record total of 400 train miles being run. This represented a total of 32 trains leaving and 32 arriving at Snow Hill.

The years between 1907 and 1912 were singularly uneventful for the J.E.R. Whether the 4 per cent ordinary dividend paid in 1896 had continued unchanged year after year is not known, but at any rate it was repeated in 1912. When preparing Volume I the writer was extremely fortunate in having access to the J.R. & T. minute books, annual reports and balance sheets. Not unnaturally, he took all possible steps to obtain the loan of similar records in respect of the J.E.R., but has been told on the highest authority that all the minute books were destroyed and, unfortunately, no annual reports have so far been forthcoming. For reasons best known to the company's officials it was only occasionally that a detailed report of the proceedings of the annual general meetings appeared in the local newspapers, and indeed, many months or even years often passed without more than casual reference to the company's activities—partly, perhaps, because the service itself was not always advertised.

For lack of any detailed information, therefore, there is no alternative but to skip the years of World War I and jump to 21 May 1919, when a joint meeting of the boards of the J.E.R. and J.R. & T. was held to petition the States to allow an increase in fares to 1½d. a mile second class and 2½d. a mile first class. The Bill was passed by the States on 26 June, and gave permission for the new fares to be in operation for a period of six years.

The Jersey *Morning News* stated in February 1925 that they understood that a number of "Halts" were shortly to be built on the J.E.R. It is not generally known that, in fact, a halt was built near Pontorson Lane, between Samarès and Le Hocq. In addition, a new station was opened at Le Bourg on 12 March 1925 by one of the company's directors in the absence, through indisposition, of the Lieutenant-Governor. Three special carriages were attached to the rear of the 2 o'clock ordinary train from St. Helier on the date in question and uncoupled at Pontac, being then backed to Le Bourg by a beflagged engine which had followed the train from St. Helier. The "special" left for Town with the directors and a good number of the general public anxious to patronise the first train.

At the 55th annual general meeting held in February 1926 the then chairman of the board, Mr. J. H. Wimble, presided. He announced that receipts were £200 higher than for the previous year and expenses £200 lower, thereby enabling the ordinary dividend to be increased to 4 per cent. The rolling stock depreciation fund stood at £8,754, which was just over two-thirds of the original cost and none too great considering the age of some of the engines and carriages—and, of course, not that he mentioned this, the fact that costs of construction were several times as much as they were originally. The fund was being added to at the rate of £400 a year. There had been an increase of 22,000 passengers over the total of the previous year.

The manager, Major Gilbert More (the father of the well-known film actor), in referring to a railcar which the company had on order, stated that he would like six of these cars on the service and not only one. He also referred to the recent installation of electric light in the passenger carriages and drew attention to the considerable saving in cost that could confidently be expected.

In spite of the favourable results recorded in 1925, the J.E.R. had had to fight against fierce bus competition on the part of the Jersey Bus Company and a Mr. Thullier, whose service was acquired by the J.E.R. in May 1926. The new arrangements came into operation on the 14th of that month, when the following advertisement appeared in the *Evening Post*:—

JERSEY EASTERN RAILWAY
MOTOR BUS SERVICE

A Service of Motor Buses is now running between Snow Hill Station and La Rocque and Fauvic. A NEW TIMETABLE will be run on and after FRIDAY, May 14th 1926. Pocket Time Tables may be obtained free from any railway station.

Features of the new service will be:

A Lunch Bus from Snow Hill every day at 1.5 p.m. for Greve d'Azette, Le Hocq and La Rocque. Returning to Town from La Rocque Inn at 1-30 p.m. :

An augmented Saturday Service.

Reduced return fares. RETURN BUS TICKETS are available on any train. Railway tickets are NOT available on the Buses.

A Bus from Snow Hill every Tuesday and Friday for the JERSEY ASYLUM at 2-30 p.m. Return fare 1s. 6d.

Fares:—					Single	Return
St. Helier to Greve d'Azette lighthouse	......	......	......		2d.	—
St. Helier to Le Hocq Hotel		......	......	......	3d.	5d.
St. Helier to Le Bourg Station	......	......	......	......	4d.	6d.
St. Helier to La Rocque Inn	......	......	......	......	5d.	8d.
St. Helier to Fauvic	......	......	......	......	6d.	10d.

ALL BUSES START FROM SNOW HILL STATION.

Please ask for new timetable now.

RAILWAY BUSES ARE RED

Unfortunately the bus service does not seem to have been much of a success and in any event 1926 was an extremely bad year for the J.E.R., a net loss of £853 being recorded as compared with a profit of £1,710 during the previous year. After taking £1,000 from reserve and paying the preference dividend there remained the sum of £317 to be carried forward.

The Sentinel steam railcar referred to by Major More arrived from London on 3 July 1927 by the steamer *Foam Queen*. It was shipped in sections, which were landed on the following day by the 30-ton crane at the half-tide steps of the Albert Pier. The car was partially assembled by a gang of workmen, placed on special sets of wheels and towed by one of the States' steam rollers on 8 July via Colomberie, Don Road, Plat Douet Road and Grève d'Azette to Georgetown, where a new siding had been built on the site of the old George Town station. There the assembly was completed and the car got into working order. In spite of the fact that Major More made no mention of this, a second car followed soon afterwards. The writer has been informed that on occasions one of the ordinary carriages was used as a trailer; prior to the introduction of the railcars trains consisting of a loco-motive and one carriage were sometimes run during the slack part of the day.

On 7 August 1928 the board of the J.R. & T. considered a letter from the J.E.R. proposing that the two concerns should amalgamate. The matter was given careful consideration but, not surprisingly, was turned down. Soon afterwards the J.E.R. was in contact with a Mr. Hunter, who proposed to acquire a controlling interest in the company and electrify the system. He was stated to have intended to be present at the annual general meeting on 27 February 1929 and to have been prevented by indisposition. Whether or not this was just an excuse is not known, but nothing more was heard of the matter.

Major Wilfred Falle, the new chairman of the company, presided and drew attention to a loss on the year's working of £707. To what extent the chairman took the shareholders into his confidence is not known, but it must have been evident by then that the company was doomed. In fact, we need only jump to 21 June 1929, when both the railway and the company's bus service closed down for good. The *Evening Post* of 22 June reported as follows:—

"The wailing of a whistle through the moonlight night was the swan song of the Jersey Eastern Railway last evening as the 10-30 rail car from Gorey Pier passed along the line on its last journey under the aegis of that company, for it was the final run after 57 useful years' service.

"Crowds of people who had used the line for business or pleasure gathered at each station and many of the level crossings to say 'Farewell' and the run took the aspect almost of a funeral procession, for many people were deeply affected.

"Quite a number, many of whom, by the way, were not regular users of the service, made the last trip as a souvenir . . . and as the car entered the terminus many an expression of regret was heard at the thought that the final run was over and the the J.E.R. service was no more."

On 22 June the Royal Court registered a resolution that the affairs of the company should be placed in voluntary liquidation and five liquidators appointed, Counsel having submitted that as the J.E.R. Co. Ltd., had been created by a special Act of the States, the proper procedure was to apply to the Court for an Act. The bailiff stated that it was with regret that the Court learned that liquidation had become inevitable. The procedure adopted by the company was perfectly correct. The dissolution would date from today, and the company would proceed to liquidate its affairs.

At a meeting held on 6 December 1932 the liquidator, Mr. Alex E. Picot, submitted a detailed statement of receipts and payments. Moveable items and rolling stock had fetched £1,502, railway track £2,383 and land and premises £23,261. Unsecured creditors were paid 1s. 6d. in the £1 after the debenture holders had been repaid the outstanding sum of £28,773. Unfortunately for them, the preference and ordinary shareholders received nothing.

Demolition had been undertaken by Dover Industries Ltd., who started operations in November 1929 the locomotives and much other metal being shipped to Poland as scrap. Of the remainder, there was a final winding-up sale in May 1930 when one of the principal items was "a well-constructed shelter over Snow Hill platform, 198 feet in length, 25 feet wide, built with 8 inch x 4 inch and 3 inch x 5 inch steel girders, which are supported by 28 ornamental cast iron columns of 15 inch circumference with artistic arches and brackets. The roof is matchboarded, felted and corrugated, with a double run of 160 feet of frosted glass (4 feet x 14 inches being the dimensions of each pane) in the centre". This was the roof that was erected in 1897 at a cost of £1,500.

It remains to mention that Snow Hill railway station was opened as a bus terminus on 18 July 1935 and undoubtedly, for a time, did much to solve St. Helier's traffic problems. On 19 March 1964 the buses were transferred to the Weighbridge and the terminus has become a car park. The turntable near where the buffer stops used to be was built for turning buses and does not date back to railway days.

Locomotives

It is a remarkable fact that during the period of nearly 56 years when the J.E.R. was in operation, only five locomotives and two steam railcars were employed. As already stated, the first two locomotives arrived in the Island on 27 April 1873, were 0-4-2 tanks built by Kitson & Co. of Leeds, and were named *Caesarea* and *Calvados*. They had coupled wheels 4 feet in diameter, trailing wheels 3 feet, a wheelbase of 12 feet 4 inches and cylinders 13 inches in diameter by 20 inches stroke.

When the line was first opened, and until 1891 or later, the locomotives ran smokebox first towards Gorey, but it was found that the top of the firebox was liable to become uncovered on the steep incline from St. Luke's to Snow Hill. Further, it is generally accepted that a tank engine runs slightly better forwards than backwards. It was therefore decided during the 1890's to turn the engines round and let them run bunker first to Gorey. There is no evidence to show that *Carteret*, which was built in 1898, ever ran otherwise than in the latter manner. There was a turntable at Green Street depot, but as far as is known its only use during the present century was for turning carriages (whose wheelbase was too long for them to be turned by orthodox means, so one end had to be supported on jacks).

On ordinary occasions between 1873 and 1891 the service could be undertaken by one engine in steam but during, for example, the horse racing at Gorey in June 1876 trains left St. Helier at 11 a.m.—11-20 —11-40—12 noon—12-20—12-40 and 1 p.m. The company only possessed two engines at that time and the turn round at each end must have been quite hectic. It is not known whether the trains proceeded to what later became known as Gorey Village station or only to Grouville, but in either case they could have stopped at few if any of the intermediate stations as "all stations" trains were allowed 19 minutes to Grouville and 22 to Gorey. The journey must have been performed in approximately 14 or 15 minutes to allow the engine to be uncoupled, run round the train, recoupled and leave again only 20 minutes after the departure from Town, and so on.

On 28 June 1877 the *Caesarea* broke down at Les Marais owing to a choked injector. The driver uncoupled the engine and managed to proceed slowly to George Town, where adjustments had to be made before further progress was possible. In due course the engine managed to limp home. Unfortunately the other engine was being overhauled at the time and in consequence wagonettes had to be provided by the company to take passengers to and from Gorey and the intermediate stations.

To avoid a repetition of a similar nature, the J.E.R. took delivery of the 2-4-0 tank *North Western* from the Jersey Railway on 21-22 June 1878. The *British Press and Jersey Times* reported: "Yesterday about 5 p.m. its removal was commenced and at a quarter to three this afternoon the engine had reached the junction of Grenville-street with Colomberie. Progress was naturally very slow; a line of rails was laid down for a few yards on which the engine travelled, and then it was relaid and a fresh move made. Some little embarrassment to the public traffic was caused by its journey, but the measures taken by the company were well carried out, and the inconvenience was reduced to a minimum."

The opinion has been expressed by other writers that the *North Western* never ran for the J.E.R. but this is not correct. On 18 May 1882 the *Calvados* broke down near Samarès. "Steam was got up in the engine *North Western*, after which the engine went to Samarès and brought back the *Calvados* and several of the occupants of the 5 o'clock train who had remained in the carriages." Again, on 11 June 1882 "one of the tubes of the boiler of the engine *North Western* burst and put out the fire, which necessitated a delay till a second engine was got ready and despatched to Gorey".

So far as is known *North Western* was withdrawn from service in 1898. According to various reports she was never a satisfactory engine, and one of the old drivers, Mr. Cabot, told a friend of the writer's that there was often difficulty in stopping her at the various stations—probably because it had not been considered worth while fitting steam brakes. She is believed to have been sold to a quarry in Scotland, but whether at once or at a later date is not known. It may be added that Mr. Cabot died in 1960 at the age of at least 80.

A fourth locomotive, the *Mont Orgueil*, was placed in service in 1886 and was almost identical with the two pioneers except that it had outside bearings to the trailing wheels, round-topped tanks and sloping firebars. It also had Naylor safety valves, but these were replaced in 1899 by others of the more familiar Ramsbottom pattern. The fifth locomotive, *Carteret*, appeared in 1898 and enabled *North Western* to be withdrawn. She reverted to inside bearings but the round-topped tanks were repeated. A few months previously *Caesarea* and *Calvados* had been reboilered with boilers 3 feet 4⅞ ins. in diameter, to conform with those of *Mont Orgueil* and *Carteret*, in place of the 3 feet boilers originally fitted.

In the account of the opening of Le Bourg station in 1925 it was mentioned that the special train back to Town was drawn by *Calvados*, which had been "in constant service between Gorey and St. Helier for 53 years and during that time had covered over a million miles in passenger work".

Messrs. Kitson & Co. of Leeds, the builders of all four 0-4-2 tanks, have kindly supplied the following dimensions of the locomotives at the time of their completion:—

	CAESAREA	CALVADOS	MONT ORGUEIL	CARTERET
Date built	1872	1872	1886	1898
Works No.	1832	1833	2972	3800
Coupled wheels (diam.)	4 ft.	4 ft.	4 ft.	4 ft.
Trailing wheels diam.)	3 ft.	3 ft.	3 ft.	3 ft.
Wheelbase	12 ft. 4 ins.	12 ft. 4 ins.	12 ft. 4 ins.	12 ft. 4 ins.
Cylinders	13 x 20 ins.	13 x 20 ins.	13 x 20 ins.	13 x 20 ins.
Boiler diameter	3 ft.	3 ft.	3 ft. 4⅞ ins.	3 ft. 4⅞ ins.
Boiler length of barrel	9 ft. 7 ins.	9 ft. 7 ins.	9 ft. 9 ins.	9 ft. 7 ins.
Heating surface, tubes	452 sq. ft.	452 sq. ft.	486 sq. ft.	454 sq. ft.
Heating surface, firebox	52 sq. ft.	52 sq. ft.	50 sq. ft.	51 sq. ft.
Total	504 sq. ft.	504 sq. ft.	536 sq. ft.	505 sq. ft.
Grate area	8.7 sq. ft.	8.7 sq. ft.	9.9 sq. ft.	8.8 sq. ft.
Working pressure	140 lb.	140 lb.	140 lb.	140 lb.
Side tanks (capacity)	536 gls.	536 gls.	570 gls.	570 gls.
Weight in working order	24 tons	24 tons	25 tons	25 tons

At the Annual General Meeting in 1926 the chairman mentioned that three of the four locomotives had been reboilered since the War and that these new boilers should at any rate last for another

12-14 years. The boiler of the remaining engine was at that time under repair at Leeds, the anticipated cost being a little over £300.

The writer is indebted to Mr. P. J. Le Gros, latterly in charge of the engine and carriage sheds at St. Helier for the information that *Calvados* (which he considered to be the best all-round engine) was condemned about 1927—that is to say at approximately the time when the railcars were introduced. This was probably the engine whose boiler was under repair a year or so previously.

The cylindrical sand-boxes on the boilers between the domes and the safety valves gave the locomotives an unusual appearance. One of the accompanying photographs shows *Mont Orgueil* without a sand box. The reason for its removal is not known but the concensus of opinion seems to be that this took place during the last year or so of the company's existence. Like the locomotives of the J.R. & T. all were fitted with acetylene headlamps, but these were of large size instead of being comparatively small.

The livery was a lightish green lined in white. After the Armistice of 1918 it seems that a brighter green was substituted and that the lining was white, black and green. At that time the frames were chocolate; the springs of the leading wheels and the wheel centres were vermilion. At some stage the engines were unlined, but it is not known whether this was a World War I economy or whether the change took place during the closing years of the company's existence. Originally *Caesarea*, *Calvados* and *Mont Orgueil* had their names painted in large letters on the side tanks, but in due course all locomotives had brass nameplates with lettering in black.

The company was able to obtain free water from the brook at Gorey Village station, and after the extension to Gorey Pier was opened a stop for water was usually made en route to Town. There were also facilities at St. Helier, but these were only made use of when necessary.

Sentinel Railcars

The two Sentinel railcars introduced in 1927 were named *Normandy* and *Brittany* respectively, and were similar in most respects to those of the J.R. & T. except as regards gauge and that they catered exclusively for second class passengers, 52 in number. The cars were painted red.

After the line closed down in 1929, *Normandy* was purchased by the J.R. & T. for £100—a bargain if ever there was one—and had to be converted from standard to 3 feet 6 inch gauge. The body of *Brittany* was purchased by a resident of Grève d'Azette for use as a summer bungalow, and as such can still be seen to this day. The locomotive section was shipped to England and until recently was in use in a quarry near Redhill, Surrey.

During the severe winter weather of February 1929 the railcars were taken out of service for three days owing to the freezing up of the feed pipes to the boilers.

Passenger Carriages

It was announced in April 1873 that 20 passenger carriages were being imported into the Island by the J.E.R. but on the day that the line was opened for traffic it was stated that the number was 14. In 1914 the total was 17 and when the line closed down in 1929 it appears to have dropped to 12—plus, of course, the two railcars. Apart from the latter all passenger stock ran on four wheels.

Included amongst the carriages placed in service in 1873, or thereabouts, were five purchased from the London & North Western Railway. Some if not all are believed to have been built in 1850 and they remained in service until about 1913. The frame and wheels of one of them were subsequently used to carry the newly-built body of a luggage van and in this way are believed to have survived for a further 10 years.

When the Jersey Railways Company Limited changed from standard to 3 feet 6 inch gauge in 1884 four of their closed carriages, which had been built in England in 1870, were purchased by the J.E.R.

Two first class carriages of a semi-saloon type were built about 1905 by the Metropolitan Carriage & Wagon Company Ltd., ostensibly to encourage members of the Royal Jersey Golf Club to travel by train between Snow Hill and Grouville. No trace has been found of any other new construction or second-hand purchases, and if it is correct that the 1929 total of passenger carriages was 12 this may well have consisted of the two golfers' carriages, the four ex-Jersey Railways and six received from England before the line was opened in 1873. There were at least three brake carriages: one with a short van section and three second class compartments, one with two seconds and a first between them and the other with a longer brake section (fitted with look-out duckets) and two second class compartments.

Until 1925 lighting was by means of oil lamps, but in that year all the passenger carriages were converted to electricity. As in the case of the J.R. & T., the brake vans and brake compartments were fitted with letter boxes, an interesting feature being that a blue pennant was flown from the roof of the guard's van of the daily mail train, which for many years left Snow Hill for Gorey at 11-30 a.m. During the period from about 1900 to 1914 the early morning train to Town on Saturdays became known as the "Fish Train" because two brake vans were attached to the rear and at La Rocque (which, incidentally, was the busiest of the intermediate stations) were loaded with barrow-loads of fish by the accompanying fisherwomen.

Letters instead of numbers were used to distinguish one vehicle from another; all were finished in what was known as varnished teak.

Except during the early years of the company's existence the locomotives—apart from the *North Western*—were fitted with steam brakes, but there was no continuous brake and the guard at each end of the train was responsible at the appropriate time for assisting the driver by applying the hand brake. Incidentally, the *British Press and Jersey Times* of 5 September 1876 stated that a night or two previously, after a firework display in Pontac Gardens, the 10-30 p.m. special from Pontac to St. Helier consisted of 12 carriages, which were crowded with passengers. This is believed to have been the longest train ever operated and must have taxed the locomotive to the utmost to surmount the gradient leading to Snow Hill. At one time, trains of 9 or 10 carriages were fairly common.

Goods Traffic

Goods traffic was virtually non-existent and in consequence the number of goods trucks was only four. In 1877 the profit and loss account made no mention of goods traffic but the takings for cattle traffic were £71, the cattle in question being imported from France and conveyed to St. Helier for slaughter. Parcels traffic, carried by passenger train, amounted to £129.

Signals

The only semaphore signal on the system was one of ancient vintage working in conjunction with the level crossing gates at Green Street for the benefit and safety of trains or engines leaving Snow Hill terminus. There were, however, a number of old-fashioned disc signals working in conjunction with other level crossing gates. At the stations trains were flagged.

Permanent Way

Latterly, at any rate, the permanent way consisted of flat-bottomed rails weighing 70 lb. per yard, spiked direct to the sleepers.

The balance sheet for 1877 included an item of £419 for 2,943 oak sleepers to supersede an equal number of pine. As the latter had presumably been newly laid in 1873 the Jersey climate must have played havoc with them. It is interesting to note that the oak sleepers cost less than 3s. each, and that they were used to renew approximately one-eighth of the total.

Gradients

Apart from a falling gradient, variously stated to have been 1 in 45 and 1 in 59, for part of the distance from Snow Hill to St. Luke's, the line was easily graded.

Accidents

The J.E.R., like the J.R. & T., managed to steer remarkably clear of serious accidents and, in fact, the only trace that has been found of an accident involving injury to passengers was on 30 September 1881 when the engine of the 5-30 p.m. train from Gorey to St. Helier backed heavily into the train preparatory to coupling up. Mr. Clement Le Sueur, one of the directors, was in the front carriage, was thrown forward and received cuts on his face and head. Another man in the same compartment received bruises, as did two or three children.

In March 1875 an incoming train ran into the buffers at St. Helier; in June 1875 the engine of a passenger train was derailed; in July 1885 the axle of a carriage broke at Grouville; and in September 1922 an axle of the brake van snapped at Fauvic. In none of these cases were there any injuries or serious damage, and the same applied to the three mishaps, referred to in earlier pages, that occurred just before or after the opening of the railway.

On 23 June 1901 two carriages, due to be shunted into a siding, were uncoupled at Snow Hill. The driver then backed the train a few yards to enable him to run around, the result being that the uncoupled carriages started off down the incline. When the driver saw what had happened he followed as quickly as possible, whistling loudly so that the crossing keepers at Green Street and the Dicq were able to open their gates. At St. Luke's, however, the stationmaster had no time to do this and his gates were smashed to matchwood. No other damage was done.

A mishap on 19 October 1913 was due to sabotage. The end carriage of a train stored in Snow Hill station for the night was uncoupled and pushed by some persons unknown until it reached the incline when it gathered speed and proceeded almost to Grève d'Azette, demolishing on the way four sets of gates.

Conclusion

Looking back, it can be said that the failure of the Jersey Eastern Railway was inevitable, and that whatever steps might have been taken the rapid increase of motor bus and private car traffic would sooner or later have resulted in bankruptcy. There is no doubt that the J.R. & T. acted wisely in introducing railcars in 1923 and it can equally be said that the J.E.R. were too late when they did so in 1927. However, even had they entered this field four years earlier the only result would have been a slight prolonging of the agony. Then again, the J.R. & T. made a very astute move when they bought up the Jersey Motor Transport Company Ltd. in August 1928, but it is perfectly obvious that even had the purchase been made at this time by the J.E.R. and not the J.R. & T. it would have been much too late to stave off the closure that took place in June of the following year. What can and must be said is that the J.R. & T. started their own bus service as early as August 1923—only four months after the J.M.T. commenced operations—whereas the J.E.R. did not follow suit until nearly three years later. Had they done so in 1923 there is justification for believing that they would have managed to survive for, say, as long as the J.R. & T. did. However, the eventual outcome would undoubtedly have been the same.

Where the J.R. & T. certainly stole a march over the J.E.R. was in the matter of liquidation, but there were several factors in their favour, not the least of which was their ability to profit by the experience of the J.E.R. Moreover, they were the fortunate owners of the J.M.T., which was worth a lot of money to them.

Snow Hill station showing roof built in 1897

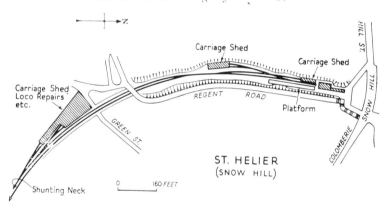

ST. HELIER
(SNOW HILL)

Carriage Shed

Carriage Shed

Carriage Shed
Loco Repairs
etc.

REGENT ROAD

Platform

GREEN ST.

COLOMBERIE

SNOW HILL

HILL ST.

Shunting Neck

0   160 FEET

N

Engine and carriage sheds at Green Street, St. Helier. On the extreme right is the main line leading to Snow Hill terminus

Up train at Grouville. The loop line and platform appear to have fallen into disuse

Societe Jersaiise

Pontac station

La Roque station

F. Foot

'Carteret' at Gorey Pier. Note acetylene headlight

Opening of Le Bourg station on 12 March, 1925

George Bird

Gorey Pier station.(Mont Orgueil Castle is prominent on the skyline)

Builder's photograph of 'Mont Orgueil' showing Naylor safety valves, outside bearings to trailing wheels and name painted on tank sides. Nameplates were provided later

'Caesarea' and demolition train at Green Street, 1929

George Bird

'Calvados' outside Green Street sheds, St. Helier

Old J.E.R. brake composite believed to have been built in England for the Jersey Railway in 1870

Old $4\frac{1}{2}$ compartment second class carriage

C. P. Baudains

Locomotive and permanent way gang in Le Hocq cutting

Old semaphore signal at Snow Hill to indicate whether or not the level crossing gates at Green Street were open.

Sentinel railcar 'Brittany' in carriage siding at Snow Hill

Emile F. Guiton

Wooden trestle bridge carrying 60 cms. gauge German line across the English Harbour, St. Helier

Metre gauge 2-6-0 T. and 0-6-0 T. locomotives in course of demolition at St. Helier, 1945

Decorated locomotive at official opening of German metre-gauge line at St. Helier, 15 July, 1942

Metre gauge German line near Wayside Stores, St. John

Metre gauge 0-6-0 T. at St. Helier. A 60 cms. gauge line can be seen on the left

J. M. David

Harbour Works Yard and lines, St. Helier, circa 1880. L.S.W.R. mail steamer 'Caledonia' at Victoria Pier. Hermitage Rock in left background

St. Helier Harbour locomotive No. 2, 'Goliath', awaiting shipment to England, 1908

Construction of Hermitage Breakwater, St. Helier Harbour. In the background is the Hermitage Rock

JERSEY EASTERN RAILWAY STATIONS

Distance (miles)		Opened	Closed
0	St. Helier (Snow Hill)	6/5/74	———
¼	St. Helier (Green Street)	7/8/73	5/5/74
½	St. Luke's	1/6/96	———
¾	George Town	about 14/8/73	31/5/96
1	Grève d'Azette	1/6/96	———
1½	Samarès	7/8/73	———
1¾	Pontorson Lane (Halt)	1925	———
2¾	Le Hocq	7/8/73	———
3	Pontac	7/8/73	———
3¾	Le Bourg	12/3/25	———
4	La Rocque	7/8/73	———
4½	Les Marais *	about 14/8/73	
	renamed Fauvic	1903	———
5	Grouville	7/8/73	———
5¾	Gorey	27/8/73	———
	renamed Gorey Village	25/5/91	———
6¼	Gorey Pier	25/5/91	———

Unless otherwise stated all stations were closed on 21/6/29.

*Les Marais station was renamed Fauvic to avoid confusion with the name Samarès.

STATISTICS

Year	Profit or Loss	Preference Dividend (per cent)	Ordinary Dividend (per cent)
1877	+ £814	nil	nil
1880	+ £1,070	nil	nil
1883	?	5	1½
1896	+ £2,271	5	4
1912	?	5	4
1925	+ £1,710	5	4
1926	− £853	5	nil
1928	− £707	nil	nil

GERMAN OCCUPATION RAILWAYS IN JERSEY

(Organisation Todt)

On 1 July 1940 German aeroplanes flew over St. Helier and the Jersey Airport, dropping copies of an ultimatum to surrender. The British Government had decided some time previously that no useful purpose would be served by defending the Island so that, in obedience to German instructions, large white flags were hoisted on all public buildings and white crosses painted at the places stipulated. A day later a German airman landed at the airport and shortly afterwards came an airborne occupation force of about 100 men. Large numbers of troops followed.

On 20 October 1941 Hitler declared that the Channel Islands would become an impregnable fortress and Mr. L. P. Sinel in his diary of *The German Occupation of Jersey* 1940-45 mentions that on 17 November 1941 there were over 40 steamers and barges in St. Helier harbour unloading stores. Thousands of foreign workers— mostly Spanish, French, Polish and Russian—were being poured into the Island to assist in the building of bunkers, gun emplacements, tunnels and sea walls. By January 1942 great fortifications were going up in all parts of the Island and "funny little railways have been constructed for these operations, particularly at Gorey and La Pulente". It was far from easy to ascertain what was going on and very inadvisable to appear inquisitive; so far as is known no official records have been kept so it has been necessary to piece together the various scraps of available information.

The principal ingredients required for the fortifications were sand, granite chippings, cement, water and, of course, reinforcing metal. Transport of the first two presented a considerable problem and was largely responsible for the building of the railways.

It was soon decided that the best sand for fortification purposes came from Grouville Bay, and to begin with a large fleet of requisitioned lorries was loaded by hand from the slipway in Gorey village. In January 1942 the railway mentioned by Mr. Sinel was working on Grouville Common and on a stretch of beach opposite and to the south of Fort William; the track was of the well-known De-cauville type, the gauge being 60 centimetres (1 foot 11¾ inches). The motive power to begin with consisted of two Deutz diesel locomotives, each capable of hauling a train of 10 trucks, which were loaded by a mechanical shovel. They had side-tipping mechanism and the sand was dumped near the former Jersey Eastern Railway's Gorey village station, whence much of it was loaded into lorries. By degrees, however, an immense quantity was allowed to accumulate.

Amongst the first fortifications to be built were those on the west side of the Island in the vicinity of La Pulente, at the southern end of St. Ouen's Bay, and in due course work was proceeding throughout the length of the bay—hence the other railway mentioned by Mr. Sinel.

The Metre Gauge Lines (3 feet 3 inches)

It will be convenient to jump ahead and quote in full Mr. Sinel's entry for 15 July 1942:—

"What must rank as one of the greatest jokes of the Occupation took place today. With all solemnity the Germans officially opened the new railway which at present connects the piers with Millbrook. A special platform was erected and speeches were made by various German officials, the military commandant of the Channel Islands blowing a whistle for the train to start and the latter cutting a decorated tape as it commenced its journey. A band enlivened the proceedings, and afterwards the officials adjourned to the Pomme d'Or Hotel for a special commemorative dinner. The Germans declare that is it only the beginning of a railway which is in due course to run right

round the Island, and that although for the moment it will be used solely for the transport
of material and troops, later on it will be available for the use of civilians and supplies for
the civil population. And to think that we scrapped our trains because they were out of
date."

Apparently the line from St. Helier to Millbrook had been opened
unofficially some weeks previously as a diary entry in May 1942 stated
that in order to save petrol barges were being loaded at Gorey harbour
with sand brought by rail from Grouville Common. They then
proceeded to St. Helier harbour, where the sand was discharged into
railway trucks, which were drawn by steam locomotives to various
points along St. Aubin's Bay.

On 18 July 1942 the *Deutsche Inselzeitung*, the official German-
language newspaper of Jersey, contained a long account of the opening
of the railway three days previously. The following is a translation
of the most interesting part:—

"It was practical rather than historical considerations that induced the German
commandant of Jersey and the commander of the fortress-building pioneers to draw up
plans for an Island railway and, after many initial difficulties had been overcome, arrange
for it to be brought into operation by the Organisation Todt. The need for transporting
building materials and guaranteeing supplies for the troops stationed in the more distant
parts of the Island were the principal reasons for proceeding with the scheme.

"The town and the harbour of St. Helier have been brought nearer to the far-away
spots. What that means can only be appreciated by those who, during the course of
route marches, have actually had experience of distances in Jersey which, on the other hand
seems to be a mere pin-point on the map of Europe. Although at first traffic would be
confined in the main to the transport of materials and troop supplies, and although the
country terminus at present bears the name St. Aubin, the day will come when it will be
possible to travel by train from the outlying parts in the north, west and east of the Island
to St. Helier with its exciting city life (*sic*), and after a comfortable railway journey reach
the harbour and the ship in readiness for a spell of home leave.

"That the railway development of Jersey is making rapid progress will be apparent
from the fact that the line to St. Aubin, after overcoming serious difficulties in a stretch
of some 120 metres, will reach Corbiere within a fortnight; that completion of the section
from Ronez to St. Mary's Church can be expected at the end of next week, and that
another stretch from La Pulente to Thiebaut will soon connect the entire west coast with
the interior."

The metre gauge line from St. Helier to St. Aubin and Corbière
can be said to have started opposite Commercial Buildings, within a
stone's throw of the former J.R. & T. Weighbridge terminus, but in
effect this was only a shunting spur for the line that proceeded along
the west side of the New North Quay. On the east of the latter was
another line which made a trailing junction with the spur, after
which there was a sharp right-hand curve opposite the entrance to
the Albert Pier, where it was joined by a branch running the entire

length of the pier. Soon afterwards a sharp left-hand curve led to the Esplanade. From West Park to St. Aubin's tunnel the roadbed of the former J.R. & T. was more or less followed. The line was single throughout except for an occasional crossing loop.

A branch crossed Victoria Avenue at Millbrook to an ordnance depot in what later became known as the "Circus Field", but has since been built over. And another branch from a point midway between Bel Royal and Beaumont was responsible for two or three houses being demolished to enable it to curve sharply to the right, cross the main road (A.1) and proceed along the Perquage Walk to an electricity station built at Tesson Mill. Sidings led from Perquage Walk to an ordnance yard on Goose Green marsh.

A blast wall had already been built at the eastern end of the old J.R. & T. tunnel at St. Aubin as a protection for the extensive galleries which were being excavated. The bore of the tunnel itself had been greatly increased and the galleries driven through solid rock, the area covered being second only to that of the much better-known German Underground Hospital, to which rather surprisingly no connecting railway was laid. In consequence of the blast wall it was impossible for the through line to proceed via the tunnel and the resulting deviation followed the railbed that was in use up to the opening of the tunnel for traffic in 1898. However, the large-scale works in the tunnel and galleries made it extremely desirable to have a direct communication with the new railway, and a siding led from the tunnel to trailing points a few yards beyond the western end. The rails in the tunnel itself were embedded in concrete and in consequence are still in existence today. Except for a few feet of mixed metre and 60 centimetres track near Les Maltières, it is believed to be the only surviving length of metre gauge track in Jersey. For the remainder of the distance to Corbière the line followed the roadbed of the old J.R. & T.

So far nothing has been said about the steps taken by the Germans to make the necessary quantities of crushed granite available for fortification purposes. This vital component was by no means overlooked by them and at a very early stage the Todt Organisation took over Ronez Quarry, the largest in the Island and situated more or less in the middle of the north coast. One of the first things they did was rebuild the "funicular", 300 yards long, from the foot of the quarry workings to the top of the cliff, 250 yards above. A truck had been allowed—as likely as not deliberately—to run amok down the incline, at the foot of which it demolished the weighbridge hut and seriously injured a number of Organisation Todt foremen who were inside. The replacement included a trolley which carried two side-tipping quarry wagons to the summit on each journey. A primary crusher was constructed in close proximity to the summit, the stone being carried thence on rubber conveyors to two gyratory crushers. It was then screened into various sizes, the overhead bins having traps underneath so that it could be loaded direct into railway trucks.

Mr. Sinel's diary entry for 30 April 1942 stated: "everywhere foreign workers are working on railroads (one from Ronez to St. Peter)". This was the same line that the German newspaper correspondent stated would be opened in July 1942 from Ronez to St. Mary's Church. It had been decided many months previously that Ronez Quarry should supply all or certainly the greater part of the Island's requirements of crushed granite and a railway to transport it was a natural sequel. It is undoubtedly true to say that to begin with Ronez was regarded by the Germans as second only in importance to St. Helier as a focal point for the Island's railway network. In fact, it is quite possible that there would have been no railways larger than 60 centimetres gauge had it not been necessary to move large quantities of crushed granite from Ronez to various parts.

The railway started at Ronez as a double line underneath the crushers and bins and was built to metre gauge (3 feet 3 inches). There were one or two sidings in the vicinity for storing trucks, but the line proper was single track except for an occasional passing loop. Upon leaving the quarry premises the line crossed what became the Route du Nord but was then merely a rough track and was laid on a substantial embankment across Mr. Renouf's sandpit. Proceeding due south through fields to Le Catelet, where further extensive earthworks were necessary to cross a valley, the line made a sharp right hand turn and passed in front of the Wayside Stores on the north side of the Route de Saint Jean (B.33), the grass verge being used where possible although in places the line ran in an adjacent field. Beyond Eden House the road was crossed diagonally and the line continued along the south side of B.33, passing St. Mary's School and Parish Hall, having crossed one or two side turnings on the level but there were, of course, no gates. It then bore slightly left through fields, where there was a siding for the 2-6-0 tank engine, which usually worked the Ronez-Les Augerez section, to be stabled. Skirting St. Mary's Arsenal, the line crossed B.53, went through more fields, making a gradual approach to B.32, which was crossed diagonally near Carrefour-a-Cendre. It then proceeded in fields closely parallel to and to the west of B.69, passing St. Peter's House, crossing B.68 and, 100 yards or so further on, trespassing into the front garden of a cottage, crossing B.69 and, for half a mile or more, continuing in fields a few feet to the west of the Rue de la Hague. After this the line curved gently to the right, passed through a gap in a granite wall—the subsequent repair is still noticeable—close to "Nonpareil", the home of the late Mr. W. H. Dickson, for many years manager of the J.R. &T. (see Volume I), crossed St. Peter's main road (A.12), passed close to where the Catholic church recently stood, bore left in a wide sweep to cross what is now the airport approach road (B.36) and soon afterwards skirted the west side of the lake in the grounds of the Mermaid Hotel (formerly the Welby Country House Hotel). Then along a rough track to Saut Falluet, in fields again for a quarter of a mile, beside a lane for 100 yards to the Pont du Val, where B.43 was crossed, and so to a length of embankment wide enough to accommodate a crossing loop. From here the line descended steeply to Pont Marquet, where it crossed B.25 and joined the Corbiere-St. Helier line by a trailing junction.

The distance from Ronez Quarry to Pont Marquet was six miles. At the latter point it was 150 feet above sea level whereas only $\frac{3}{8}$ mile previously it had been 225 feet, the average gradient on this stretch being 1 in 26. About $\frac{3}{4}$ mile further back still the height had been 275 feet, the average gradient in this case being the relatively easy one of 1 in 80. The loaded trains from Ronez had a mainly downhill journey, but two locomotives were always employed to provide adequate braking power; the usual load was about 20 trucks. All long trains proceeding from St. Aubin to Ronez, even if empty, had a banking engine at the rear.

The junction at Pont Marquet gave access to many spots in the vicinity of Corbière where heavy fortifications were under way, but it did not help much with many others in the vicinity of the Five Mile Road, bordering St. Ouen's Bay. It was decided, therefore, to build a branch line—starting more or less from the spot where "Mon

Sejour", Les Augerez, now stands. Here there were already sidings and an ordnance yard.

The roadbed continued to Les Marrettes (later known as "Red Roofs"), having proceeded in a westerly direction for about a quarter of a mile and then veering to the south-west to reach the grounds of La Hougue, which border the main road from St. Peter to St. Ouen (A.12). Instead of a level crossing, as there had been in many places on the sections already described, a tunnel was built in concrete under the road. Thenceforth the line followed the Val-de-la-Mare and further on much of it has been covered by the waters of the new reservoir. Beyond the dam, and beside Bethesda Chapel, the line crossed C.106 by a concrete overbridge of 17 feet span and 14 feet high, this being followed by a long embankment, the material for which was obtained from anti-invasion canals which the Germans dug in the vicinity. The bridge still exists but that part of the embankment immediately adjacent to it has been removed.

Despite what has been said in the past, it seems certain that not only was the track of this Val-de-la-Mare line duly laid but that it consisted of a mixed gauge of one metre and 60 centimetres. Various people distinctly remember seeing the line in operation, and in fact on one Sunday the entire congregation of Bethesda Chapel witnessed a steam engine passing over the bridge and vanishing up the valley. It does seem, however, that these lines were not used very much and not for long.

To give some indication of the topography of the line, the distance from "Mon Sejour" to the Five Mile Road is approximately $2\frac{1}{2}$ miles. At the former the line was 300 feet above sea level and at the latter only 25 feet, which means that the average gradient was 1 in 48. However, there was a fairly level stretch at the top end and also from Les Marrettes to the Five Mile Road so that in a distance of one mile two furlongs from the vicinity of La Hougue to the position of the present dam there was a fall of 200 feet, giving an average gradient of 1 in 28. Here again the loaded trains were proceeding downhill. The task of drawing the trucks up the hill was about the same as that on the steepest part of the "main" line.

Before passing on to the 60 centimetre lines mention must be made of the uncompleted metre gauge Les Landes line, which started near the artillery battery at Les Landes, crossed the front garden of Les Landes House, past the farm known as "Longfield", just to the south of what is now St. George's Estate, straight through the fields of the L'Etocquet area, over the main road La Grande Route de Vichelez between Les Six Boules and Leoville, through the front garden of "La Chasse", across Le Chemin de l'Eglise and petered out about $\frac{1}{4}$ mile to the east of what is now the States Telecommunications Centre. The probable reason for the abandonment of the line is that work on the construction of the artillery battery at Les Landes was completed before the line which was to serve it. No locomotive ever ran on the line—only a hand-powered gangers' trolley.

The 60 Centimetres Gauge Lines (1 foot $11\frac{3}{4}$ inches)
(a) West Coast

The German account of the opening ceremony on 15 July 1942 mentioned a section of line from La Pulente to La Thiebaut (L'Etacq), and stated that the entire west coast would soon be connected with the interior—by means of the metre gauge line just described. At this time the intention was undoubtedly for Ronez Quarry to supply all the crushed granite needed in the west.

At the foot of the Mont Pinel stood two quarries, known as L'Etacq and La Thiebaut. Crushing and screening plant was built by the Germans from scratch—probably because they began to realise that the capacity of Ronez was insufficient to meet the requirements of the entire Island (and for the same reason a third quarry was opened near the east coast).

A 60 centimetres gauge line started at these quarries, following a course slightly to the north of the Route des Laveurs, which it crossed before reaching the Blue Dahlia (since completely rebuilt as the New Mediterranean), passed in front of it and ran along the grass verge of the Five Mile Road to a point just beyond the Watersplash, where it crossed the road diagonally, proceeding in the fields on the sea side of the road. The line terminated nearly opposite La Pulente Hotel. Present-day traces are few, but until comparatively recently there was a yard of track embedded in the side of the road opposite the A.A. Box and Peacock Farm. There were numerous temporary branches along the line, laid in and subsequently removed as and when required. Most important of all, there was a triangular junction in the neighbourhood of Peacock Farm, enabling trains to or from both La Thiebaut and La Pulente to proceed direct to or from Les Marrettes

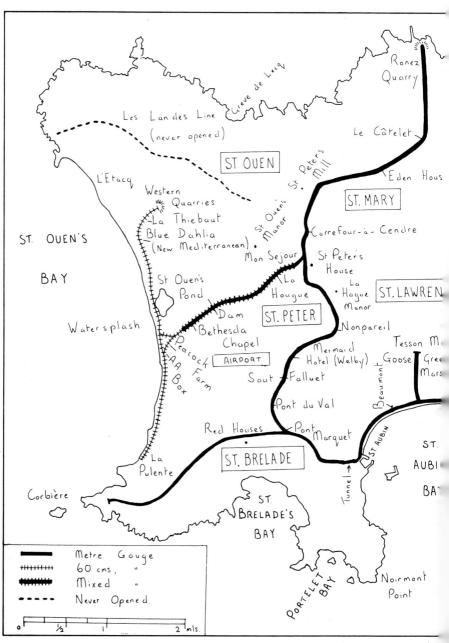

Grève de Lecq

Ronez
Quarry

Les Landes Line
(never opened)

Le Câtelet

ST OUEN

St Peter's Mill

Eden Hous

L'Etacq

Western
Quarries
La Thiebaut
Blue Dahlia
(New Mediterranean)

St Ouen's Manor

ST. MARY

Carrefour-à-Cendre

ST. OUEN'S

BAY

Mon Sejour

St Peter's
House
La
Hague
Manor

ST. LAWREN

St Ouen's
Pond

La
Hougue

Watersplash

Dam
Bethesda
Chapel

ST. PETER

Nonpareil

Peacock Farm

AIRPORT

Mermaid
Hotel (Welby)

Tesson M
Goose Gree
Mars

AA Box

Saut — Falluet

Pont du Val

Beaumont

Red Houses

Pont
Marquet

ST. AUBIN

ST.
AUBI
BA

La
Pulente

ST. BRELADE

Tunnel

Corbière

ST.
BRELADE'S
BAY

Noirmont
Point

PORTELET BAY

	Metre Gauge
┼┼┼┼┼	60 cms. "
▆▆▆	Mixed "
- - - -	Never Opened

0   ½   1   2 mls.

GERMAN LINE

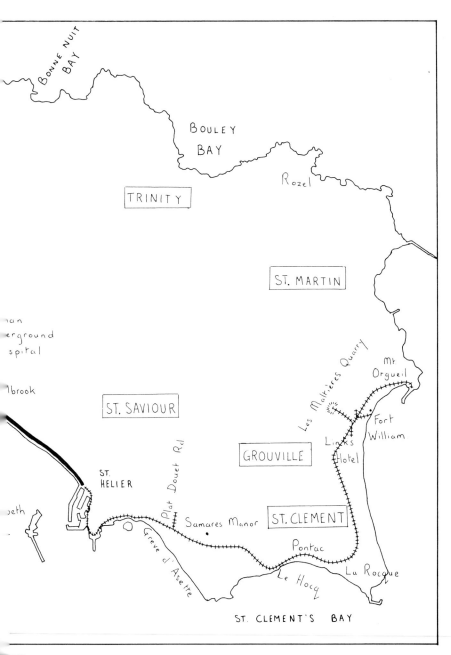

BONNE NUIT BAY

BOULEY BAY

Rozel

TRINITY

ST. MARTIN

ʌan
erground
spital

Ibrook

ST. SAVIOUR

Les Matrières Quarry

Mt Orgueil

Fort William

Links Hotel

GROUVILLE

ST. HELIER

Plat Douet Rd

Samares Manor

ST. CLEMENT

eth

Greve d' Asette

Pontac

La Rocque

Le Hocq

ST. CLEMENT'S BAY

("Red Roofs"), which was the western terminal of the metre gauge line as well as the locality of the engine sheds for both gauges. As already stated, there was a mixed gauge line from Les Marrettes via the Val-de-la-Mare to Les Augerez.

An aerial photograph taken in April 1943 shows at least five trains at work along the length of the Five Mile Road. Steam as well as diesel motive power was used on this section.

The 60 Centimetres Gauge Lines (1 foot 11¾ inches)
(b) East Coast

The 60 centimetres gauge lines at Grouville and Gorey, already referred to, were probably the first German lines, irrespective of gauge, to be laid in the Island, were what are often described as con-tractor's lines and their object was to collect sand from the beach in the vicinity of Fort William and deliver it to the dump near the former Gorey Village station, whence it was delivered by lorry to many parts of the Island.

By March 1942 a second mechanical shovel was in operation and further lines had been laid. Soon afterwards a wooden sand tip was constructed beside the Gorey New Road opposite Fort William to expedite the loading of lorries. A maximum of four trucks at a time could be pushed up the ramp to the tip.

By July 1942 sand was being loaded in barges at Gorey harbour, conveyed to St. Helier and there transhipped to the railway that already stretched to Millbrook and beyond. To facilitate these oper-ations the 60 centimetres gauge line was extended from the vicinity of Fort William along the surface of the road to Gorey Pier. In the opposite direction a second sand dump was started on Grouville Common not far from the former Links Hotel and resulted in further railway extensions.

Just as important as sand in the building of the fortifications was a plentiful supply of crushed granite. As already stated the original intention was for Ronez Quarry to supply the entire Island but in due course the Western Quarries at La Thiebaut were started and a crushing plant built. On the east side of the Island Les Maltieres Quarry had been lying derelict for some considerable time. It was decided as early as May 1942 not only to reopen it but extend it greatly and build a crushing plant, one of the mechanical shovels hitherto used on the beach being transferred to the quarry.

At that time it had been decided to build a railway from Gorey to St. Helier, but it had not been decided whether the gauge should be one metre or 60 centimetres. In consequence a short length of line at the crushing plant was laid in concrete to a mixed gauge—the two outer rails were metre gauge and the two inner 60 centimetres. They can still be seen to-day outside the main quarry building which, rather cleverly, has been converted into a block of somewhat unsightly flats.

For various reasons progress on the east coast did not keep pace with the west. In October 1942 Mr. Sinel reported that plans were well in hand to connect the track, which by then extended from Gorey nearly to Fauvic, with the line running from St. Helier to the west, the implication being that the whole was to be built to metre gauge. In January 1943 Mr. Sinel stated that plans had been prepared for the laying of a railway from St. Helier to Gorey, commencing at the Victoria Pier and keeping as far as possible to the track of the old Jersey Eastern Railway, but it was not until March 1943 that "the Germans have to-day started work at Grouville which seems to indicate that the laying of the railway track running to town is to be commenced". Perhaps the delay was due to arguments about the gauge. At any rate, it is time to say that on account of space considerations between St. Helier harbour and Havre-des-Pas it was wisely decided to use the 60 centimetres gauge.

On 28 April 1943 the Germans began to demolish the Abergeldie Hotel at the Dicq to make room for the line. A month later, on 26 May, "blasting has been going on at the end of the Victoria Pier, near the Harvey Monument. This is in connection with the tunnel which has been bored under Mount Bingham for the railway to run through."

At Commercial Buildings the track met "the one running from the west, but the two gauges are different". In fact, it is simplest to say that the 60 centimetres gauge started from a point adjacent to the Esplanade and opposite Castle Street, but like the metre gauge line opposite Commercial Buildings this was only a shunting spur—for the line that extended the length of the Albert Pier. There was also a connection opposite where the Victoria Monument then was with a line on the east side of the New North Quay. Reference to the map will indicate the layout of the various lines in the harbour.

After running along Commercial Buildings the line crossed the English Harbour by a wooden bridge with a lifting span to enable small craft to enter or leave. The line then ran at the back of La Folie Inn, skirted the French Harbour (a small portion of which was filled in) and soon entered the tunnel that had been bored through South Hill and ended in the yard of the Harbour Works (now the electricity generating station). The rails are still in existence in the tunnel.

It will be recalled that the entry for January 1943 stated that the line from St. Helier to the east would start at the Victoria Pier. In theory, at any rate, there was ample justification for the building of the extension line to connect with the metre gauge lines opposite Commercial Buildings, but what is rather amazing is that it was considered necessary to build the tunnel as this would have been avoided by substituting a reversing spur, with a run around for the locomotive, a short distance along Victoria Pier. The train would then have been able to proceed into the Harbour Works by the main entrance and continue within a few yards of the tunnel mouth. If traffic on the line had been at all heavy the tunnel would have been of inestimable value, but as will be seen shortly it was for the most part surprisingly light.

A left-hand curve of minimum radius brought the line to Point-des-Pas and La Collette Walk, and to reach the latter it was necessary for it to be built out seawards for a few feet. It was this tight curve, combined with the tunnel and the bridge over the English Harbour that were largely responsible for the decision to construct the line to the narrower of the two gauges.

At the end of La Collette Walk, opposite Green Street, the line took to the roadway, which it followed past the swimming pool to the Dicq where, thanks to the demolition of the Abergeldie Hotel, it was just possible to negotiate a sharp reverse curve. It then crossed the road and proceeding through the car park of the Demi-des-Pas Hotel ran on the sea side of the latter and of the Victor Hugo Hotel, regaining the road at "Baal's Corner". From there onwards it more or les followed the track of the old Jersey Eastern Railway, except at Le Hocq where building developments made it necessary to run at the side of the main road in the direction of Pontac.

The engine sheds were at Greve d'Azette. At this point a branch line proceeded northwards along Plat Douet Road to an ordnance yard on what is now the Grasett Park estate.

The line was single throughout except for occasional crossing loops and at Grouville linked up with the line running south-east from

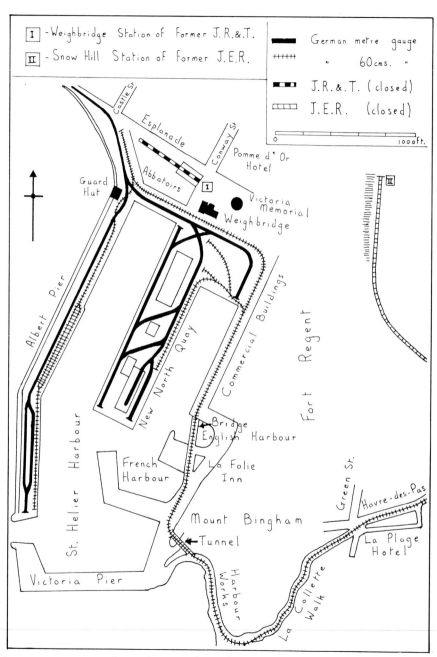

Castle St.

Esplanade

Conway St.

Pomme d' Or Hotel

Guard Hut

Abbatoirs

I

Victoria Memorial

Weighbridge

Albert Pier

New North Quay

Commercial Buildings

Fort Regent

St. Helier Harbour

French Harbour

Bridge

English Harbour

La Folie Inn

Green St.

Havre-des-Pas

Mount Bingham

La Plage Hotel

Tunnel

Victoria Pier

Harbour Works

La Collette Walk

II

German lines in and around St. Helier Harbour

Les Maltieres Quarry, the eastern terminus being at Gorey Pier. By that time the sand-collecting lines running on to the beach between Fort William and the Links Hotel had been removed.

In September 1943 Mr. Sinel reported that the number of German troops in the Island was diminishing and that large quantities of building material, concrete mixers and even railway engines, some of which had only been in the Island for a matter of weeks, were being shipped back to France. What was even more significant was that the line from Gorey to St. Helier had "hardly justified its existence, for on an average it is used about twice a week". It should, however, be added that for at least the first six weeks after it was opened it was very busy. Most of the concrete of the fortifications at Elizabeth Castle and St. Aubin's Fort contains stone brought by rail from Les Maltieres to Commercial Buildings, where it was off-loaded into barges for conveyance to its destination. Later on, during the early months of 1945 if not before, the line seems to have fallen into almost complete disuse, which perhaps was just as well as, according to many reports, a large proportion of the sleepers had been purloined for firewood!

Locomotives
(a) Metre Gauge

The first metre gauge locomotive, an 0-6-0 tank, arrived in the Island about April 1942, and was painted a khaki colour, with white swastikas and the letters "OT" (Organisation Todt) on the side tanks in readiness for the opening ceremony. It bore the number 19 and was built in 1906 by Corpet & Louvet for the Tramways de Finistere. It was acquired by a French contractor, Paul Frot, was in his yard at Sampigny in June 1940 and was commandeered by the French Army. After the Franco-German armistice it was seized by the Germans.

Other Frot locomotives to appear in Jersey were 0-6-0 tank No. 17, built by Corpet & Louvet in 1903, No. 22, an 0-8-0 tank from the same builders in 1923 (as might be expected this engine suffered frequent derailments) and a much smaller 0-4-0 tank.

A 2-6-0 tank, which worked extensively between Ronez and Les Augerez, was built in 1913 for the Chemins de Fer du Rhone et Loire. It had a hooter (still remembered by residents of St. Mary and St. John) instead of a whistle as it ran at one time on a roadside tramway, a hooter being less likely to frighten horses.

The 0-6-0 tank shown inthe illustration beside the partly demolished 2-6-0 was built in Germany by Orenstein & Koppel.

A wooden engine shed was built at St. Aubin on the site of the present ornamental gardens, and for a time after Liberation Day, 9 May 1945, most of the surviving engines were stored there. By February 1946 they had proceeded to St. Helier harbour under their own steam or were towed there by the Orenstein & Koppel. Nos. 17, 19 and 22 had been returned to France in October 1943.

It is believed that the total number of metre gauge steam engines in Jersey was 15—all of these side tanks with outside cylinders.

(b) 60 Centimetres Gauge

To begin with two Deutz diesel locomotives were responsible for hauling the loaded trucks, up to ten in number, from the beach at Grouville to the sand dump near the former Gorey Village station. At a later date three further locomotives of similar type and two smaller ones arrived, and in due course the latter were responsible for pushing trucks up the ramp to the sand tip.

For a short time two brand new Czech steam locomotives, wood burners with diamond stacks worked on the eastern lines. They are referred to in the Sinel Diary in connection with the report: "Several railway engines, some of which have only been in the Island for a few weeks, have been returned".

Rolling Stock

The metre gauge rolling stock consisted of 312 open trucks, which were commandeered from Paul Frot and handed over to the Polish firm of Gorgass, who was working for the Germans and who lost no time in erasing the Frot name and substituting PAUL GORGASS— POSEN, hence the earlier belief that the trucks were of Polish origin. Of the 312 trucks, 225 were of type 1600 with spring buffers and a capacity of four cubic metres, and 87 were of type 500 with solid oak buffers and a capacity of three cubic metres. In 1946, 128 of the 1600 type and 48 of the 500 type plus 14 open trucks and five flat trucks were reshipped to France.

The 60 centimetres stock consisted largely of side-tipping trucks.

Permanent Way

Flat-bottomed rails of varying weights and dimensions were in use for the metre gauge lines and were spiked direct to wooden sleepers. In so far as the 60 centimetres lines were concerned, some of the sleepers were of wood and some of the familiar Decauville type.

In the vicinity of St. Helier harbour the tops of the rails were level with the surface of the roadway so as to avoid interference with vehicular traffic.

Accidents

On 26 July 1942 a metre gauge engine jumped the rails on the sharp bend at the landward end of the Albert Pier and it is understood that much trouble was experienced at this spot. Elsewhere there were many minor derailments, some of which were due to stones being placed on the line by children.

On 10 June 1943 a "shocking tragedy" occurred in the fields between Ronez Quarry and Le Catelet. A farmer who was stone deaf was on the way to move some of his cows, did not hear the approach of a train, was knocked down and killed. At the subsequent inquiry a verdict of accidental death was recorded.

Six months later another local man was crushed between two trucks at Grouville when attempting to couple them together and died from his injuries.

There was also a collision at a level crossing near St. Mary's Arsenal between a German despatch rider and a train propelled by a locomotive. The rider was perhaps fortunate to lose no more than a foot.

Granite Quarries

Ronez Quarry ceased operations at the end of 1943, and work on stripping the plant down started in January 1944. The machinery was loaded into packing cases and taken by train to St. Helier in April for shipment to St. Malo, its final destination being Cherbourg. It is believed never to have arrived there.

La Thiebaut and L'Elacq also ceased work at the end of 1943. Subsequently, granite was supplied from Les Maltieres at Gorey for the east of the Island, wherever work was still going on. The needs of the west were supplied by a stone-crusher set up near the tunnels in close proximity to the Victoria Hotel in St. Peter's Valley. In this way much of the spoil from the tunnels was disposed of.

Passenger Traffic

Contrary to what was originally intended, there was never any civilian passenger traffic, but it seems clear that troops were often moved from point to point, as required, in ordinary goods trucks. As likely as not baulks of timber were supplied for them to sit on. The only specific mention of Forces' traffic occurred in the Sinel diary on 11 September 1944: "A large number of sailors, who are undergoing training, went to St. Aubin's today by train".

Finale

During the days, weeks and months following Liberation Day, 9 May 1945, there was a colossal amount of work to be performed or supervised by the British Task Force 135, including the removal of over 150 different minefields, and the collection and disposal of 30,000 tons of ammunition and of 400 guns.

The Jersey *Evening Post* of 29 September 1945 stated that work was progressing on the removal of the railway lines along La Collette Walk and from the private property beyond the Dicq, but there was no sign of their removal from the roadway in the vicinity of Havre-des-Pas and Plat Douet Road, where they were stated to be a danger, particularly to cyclists. By the end of 1945 or early in 1946 only a comparatively few traces of the railway were readily noticeable. The Railway Walk from St. Aubin to Corbière had again become a delightful haunt for pedestrians.

ST. CATHERINE'S BREAKWATER, JERSEY

Reference was made in Volume I to the commencement of work in 1847 on St. Catherine's Breakwater, on the east coast of Jersey, and to the fact that a temporary contractor's railway was used in connection therewith. Rather surprisingly, practically no information is available concerning the railway and, to make matters worse, it has not even been possible to ascertain what gauge was employed.

Between March and June 1847 600 vergees (i.e. 250 acres) of land were purchased in the parish of St. Martin and on 28 June 50 men were employed in cutting down trees near Archirondel Tower. Over 300 men and large quantities of equipment arrived from England a week later by the steamer *Princess Royal* and work started in earnest.

The *Comet* (Guernsey) of 29 July 1847 stated: "The works at St. Catherine's Bay are progressing rapidly. Operations have commenced on both sides of the bay, near Archirondel Tower and opposite the point of Verclut. About 200 workmen are employed on the former spot, where a tram road has been laid down, from the quarries about to be opened to the beach, a distance of about 600 feet. On the other side of the bay, near Verclut, about 120 men are at work, and a tram road about 200 feet long is also laid down".

The Rev. G. R. Balleine in *Bailiwick of Jersey* stated: "The first step was to join the Archirondel rock to the shore, and to do this a steam tramway was made to bring the stone to the spot. The men were then switched to the Verclut breakwater, which was run out half a mile to sea; but in 1852, before they could resume work on the Archirondel pier, which should have stretched out to meet the other, the work was suddenly stopped". The original intention was for the two parallel arms to be separated by a harbour entrance 900 feet wide, but the second arm has never been built.

The reasons for the cessation of work were that relations between Britain and France had improved greatly and that the increasing use of steam for large men-of-war made it no longer necessary to build a naval port in close proximity to the coast of France, even though the ports of Cherbourg, Granville and St. Malo were at that time being greatly enlarged and improved.

St. Catherine's Bay took its name from a mediaeval chapel which stood close to the Martello Tower at Archirondel. Mr. Balleine mentioned that one wall of the chapel remained until 1852, when it was pulled down to make room for the tramway.

In 1855 there were advertisements in the *Jersey Times* for the sale of steam engines, wagons, rails, sleepers, etc., used in connection with the breakwaters, but unfortunately no details were given. St. Catherine's Breakwater was taken over by the States of Jersey in 1878.

The *British Press & Jersey Times* of 28 October 1873 stated: "Few places present greater attractions to tourists than the Island of Jersey, and fewer still possess worse accommodation for landing and embarking passengers". At that time the Victoria Pier was used by the mail steamers and was "only available at certain states of the tide. Hence, to the discomforts attendant upon the usually rough passage across the Channel is often added that of landing from the steamer in a small boat in all weather".

The decision to build a new harbour was reached by the States of Jersey on 31 March 1871. The works were to consist of a breakwater commencing on the south face of Elizabeth Castle and running therefrom across the Hermitage Rock in a southerly direction for upwards of 2,500 feet. In addition, La Collette Harbour Works, described by Philip Ahier as one of the Island "follies", were to consist of a pier commencing at Point-des-Pas and running at first in a S.W. direction and then W.N.W. for a total distance of over half a mile.

On 30 April 1874 "a new locomotive engine, for general purposes, was worked today for the first time at the new harbour works, La Collettee. It is named the *David* and seems to work satisfactorily". The builders were Messrs. Fletcher, Jennings & Co., of Whitehaven, the works number 129 and the cost £980.

Locomotive No. 2 was named *Goliath* (works No. 139) and No. 3 *Merton* (works No. 150). All three were of 3 feet gauge. They were 0-4-0 saddle tanks with outside cylinders 9 inches x 16 inches; boilers of 2 feet 9 inches. diameter; heating surface 228 square feet plus firebox 32 square feet, making a total of 260 square feet. All were products of the same builders.

On 9 December 1874 a south-westerly gale sprang up and at 5-45 a.m. at least 200 feet of the new La Collette breakwater was severely damaged, the railway lines being twisted to ribbons in places and wagons were upset. The locomotive *David* was also damaged but was again in working order by the afternoon of the 12th, by which time new track had been laid.

A second severe gale was experienced on 10 November 1875 and resulted in 300 feet of La Collette breakwater being thrown bodily out of position. "Damage was done to one of the engines used for drawing trucks. It was inverted, but this damage was trifling when compared with that done to the sea wall. The tram lines were torn up; the rails were twisted into fantastic shapes."

From this statement it would appear that more than one locomotive was used at La Collette, and as it is known that one was employed on the Hermitage Breakwater it can be assumed that two ran at the former site. As already stated, *David* was detailed to La Collette in April 1874. It is a reasonable assumption, therefore, that *Goliath*, the second arrival, would have been allotted to the Hermitage Breakwater, and if that was the case then *Merton* would have gone to La Collette.

The Hermitage Breakwater was not damaged by either of the gales and work continued without interruption. On 11 February 1876 however, the States decided to discontinue work at La Collette until the Hermitage Breakwater was sufficiently advanced to serve as a protection. Fifteen months later the foundations of the latter had been completed for a length of 1,580 feet and the work was reported a great success. On the other hand, the damage on two occasions to La Collette proved that the work there was not of sufficient strength to withstand the enormous battering it received. On 20 June 1877 it was decided that it would be in the public interest to discontinue incurring any further expense at La Collette; the total outlay there had been over £180,000.

All three locomotives were sold in 1908 to the North Devon Clay Company Ltd, after lying derelict for many years. It seems probable that the permanent way on the Hermitage Breakwater was not dismantled until considerably later as until recently there were clear signs of where sleepers had been laid.

The North Devon Clay Company owned and operated the Torrington & Marland Light Railway, which had been opened in 1880 and ran from the goods yard at Torrington station, London & South Western Railway, for a distance of about seven miles to Peter's Marland Clay Works. At the time of the purchase of the Jersey locomotives the company owned four others; it seems that for a time all three newcomers ran in their original condition. However, *The Locomotive* stated in 1913 that owing to their poor condition after a

long period of idleness at St. Helier, an engine named *Jersey* had
appeared bearing a works No. 129, which was in fact that of the
pioneer *David*. The explanation is that this locomotive was a rebuild
of parts from all three. Moreover, it had been found that the ex-Jersey
locomotives were too heavy for the 30 lb. per yard rails and engineering
works of the T. & M.L.R., so the ingenious solution was found of
removing the saddle tank from the boiler and transferring it to a
four-wheeled truck, thereby in effect making *Jersey* an 0-4-0 tender
engine. At a later date this saddle tank was replaced by a spare boiler
and in this odd form the engine remained in service until 1951, although the major portion of the T. & M. had been reconstructed to
standard gauge in 1925.

Ronez Quarry, Jersey

In 1902 the Ronez Quarries Company built a jetty at a cost of
£1,000 to facilitate the export of granite from Ronez Point, roughly
mid-way along the north coast of Jersey, to England and elsewhere.
Some years later, after at least two intermediate changes of ownership,
the business was sold to a mainland concern, the Croft Granite Brick
& Concrete Company Ltd., and in June 1913 this company was sued
by the British Treasury, who claimed from them the right to the
foreshore at Ronez. The company lost the case but the matter was
settled amicably by their agreeing to pay an annual rental.

A number of expert witnesses and others had made an official
visit to the quarry, and the writer has in his possession three photographs taken on that occasion. One shows the jetty with a network of
railway lines leading from it, another a length of narrow gauge
track that is believed to have been about 300 yards long and the third
a steam locomotive, obviously used for hauling a string of trucks. It
is understood that this locomotive (there was only one) was a Bagnall
0-4-0 ST and had been acquired in 1912 or 1913; it did not remain
in service very long and had certainly vanished from the scene of
activities by 1926 or earlier.

The flat-bottomed rails that were in use appear to have been laid
to a gauge of 2 feet, or thereabouts, those in the second photograph

resting on what appear to be standard-gauge wooden sleepers, which may perhaps have been purchased cheaply from, say, the Jersey Eastern Railway. No other information is available, but it will be seen from the chapter dealing with the Occupation lines in Jersey that the Germans built a standard-gauge "funicular" to transport granite from the workings to the crushing plant at the top of the 250 feet high cliff.

The present owners of the quarry, the Jersey Granite & Concrete Company Ltd., purchased it from the Croft Company in 1921, and have since extended it out of all recognition.

AUTHOR'S NOTE

Grateful thanks are due to Mr. L. P. Sinel for permission to quote extracts from his "Occupation Diary", which has helped considerably in completing the chapter dealing with the German lines, and to Messrs. Michael Ginns and J. Slade for a variety of information on the same subject. Mrs. R. M. Le Maistre has very kindly supplied two rare railway maps, one of which is reproduced herewith. The following (all of Jersey unless otherwise stated) have also rendered valuable assistance in one way or another:—

Messrs. G. E. Baddeley (London); C. P. Baudains; K. Benest (Surrey); Dr. P. G. Bentlif; Messrs. George Bird; F. de L. Bois; A. Brandon-Langley (London); R. G. Burt; H. Dalston (Oxon); Raymond Falle; Emile F. Guiton; F. H. Hack; Capt. E. C. Lance; Messrs. L. A. Landick; P. J. Le Gros; J. G. Le Quesne, Q.C. (London); H. P. Le Ruez; Advocate R. Lempriere; Rev. P. G. K. Manton; Messrs. G. C. Michel; Neil Pitts (Kent); R. W. Richards; P. C. Vibert; J. F. Yeates.

I hope I shall be forgiven if I have omitted anyone who ought to have been included.

Further information is required about the German locomotives used in Jersey (and for that matter in Guernsey) and any details on the subject will be most welcome, as also would further photographs of the German lines in general.

P.S. I am greatly indebted to Mr. Michael Ginns, president of the Channel Islands Occupation Society, for most of the new information about the German lines.

INDEX